7 Steps to Small Business Marketing

'Visibility, Consistency and Relatability'

Author| Speaker|Mompreneur|Marketing Connoisseur

Jamila Guyton

Jamila Guyton is a remarkable speaker, author, and mompreneur invigorating small business with passion, growth and creative marketing. As the Marketing Connoisseur, she is assisting entrepreneurs across the nation with growth and vitality. A Determined, Motivated and Successful Woman, Jamila was convinced in her 20's that she was destined for a greater life, one that provided purpose and change to those around her daily. After spending years and years in corporate America helping to build other brands through sales and marketing she is now decided to use her gifts to serve entrepreneurs in need and live the life she always imagined. She is committed and equipped to help fellow entrepreneurs intensify growth and live the life they deserve through creative effective strategy.

Jamila is a proud mompreneur and the CEO of ProSync Consulting. Through this consulting firm, she has supported numerous entrepreneurs in GROWING their businesses from the inside out. Jamila carries a marketing degree from Hampton University and has worked tirelessly to become a savvy Marketer with a knack for creating and developing creative strategies. Her clientele which consists of authors, speakers, publishers, fashion designers, beauty consultants and entrepreneurs whose business are tied to serving the world.

When Jamila set her sights on becoming an entrepreneur the one thing she was determined to do was help others. Her passion for helping others to succeed and grow is contagious. Her personality and openness allows entrepreneurs to feel right at home and fosters a partnership that is unwavering. Often times you will hear Jamila discuss her dreams of creating a conglomerate of businesses where she and everyone involved can share in the joy and excitement of sharing in each other's successes.

Passionate, empowering, creative and determined Jamila's energy inspires everyone she encounters. It is impossible to interact with her and not be ignited and stirred to take action and GROW.

Make your marketing count, and make it easy

Your marketing efforts aren't bringing in any dollars, dear. So, let's talk.

Marketing is two parts: creativity and strategy. But one without the other is like Kool-Aid with no sugar—it doesn't work).

In order for your marketing to be effective, you have to be clear on where you are heading and have the ability to set yourself apart from the crowd. In this book, I intend to give you seven steps to help you with effective marketing.

In this book I have included samples of templates to get you going. Each person that purchased the book will receive the templates by email. If you did not provide your email at purchase please email me at jamila.guyton@prosyncconsulting.com and I will send them to you ASAP.

Now Let's Get Started!

Know Yourself, Product, and Service

Step 1: Know Yourself, Product, and Service.

The first step to any marketing plan is knowing what you're selling. That sounds like common sense, right? Well, tell me how many times you have come up with an idea that you thought was amazing, but then you told someone else, and that person responded with a million questions you couldn't answer. *How does it work? How much does it cost? What is the return on Investment? How long will it take?* The list of inquiries goes on. It's OK—you're not alone. But, because this is the most important step in the plan, give it time. Do the work. Sit down and map out your *why*. What's the why? It's why you went into business; it's the problem you want to solve for others; it's the reason why you are better than the rest. There a few things I have found helpful in overcoming this step in the process. The first is sitting down and mapping out from start to finish how your product or service works. Additionally, take the time to write down all of the logical questions you can think of if you were on the other side of the coin. Once you have your questions, answer each one of them in as much detail as possible. Secondly, take what you have to your trusted circle. (Oh, wait, you didn't think you were going through this alone—NO WAY!) Having a trusted circle is important if you don't have a business coach. Try joining some entrepreneurial meetups and business groups in your area. Lastly, if you have some friends and family members you trust with your vision, then try them, as well. Be receptive to the feedback but also protective of the vision. Listen to what they say, and take copious notes. You need to go back and make sure this information matches up with what you have written down. Once you have done the evaluation, then you need to make clear decisions. If all matches, great, but more than likely there are a few things you need to tweak or change about your plan. Once you think you have it finalized and you now know your product or service like the back of your hand, it's time to move forward into the next step.

Included is a quick brand audit you can conduct with your stakeholders to be sure that everyone is on the same page about how you view your product or service and understands the overall vision for your brand.

To Whom Are You Selling? Know Your Target Market

Step 2: To Whom Are You Selling? Know Your Target Market.

How can you get business if you don't know whom you are selling to? To put it simply, not knowing your target market is like a teacher explaining multiplication to a kindergartner. Probably not the right audience. This step will be the layer on top of the foundation you built with Step 1. Knowing your audience will allow you to formulate your message and your brand. This will give you insight into all of the strategic things you need to do to execute each other step. This is the part of the process where you will need to be completely free of clutter to focus. You need to laser focus in on who they are, what they want, why you fit that need, where they shop, what they watch on television, etc. Stalk your target market. Research your target market. Survey your target market. When honing in on your target market, it is extremely important that you go back constantly to Step 1. Knowing what you sell will help push you forward into all of the next steps.

Be exclusive but inclusive. What does that mean? Find your target market, but as with anything in life, nothing is ever black and white. There are always outliers—those clients and customers who aren't in your niche but you wouldn't turn away if they requested your services or products. So, in defining your market, be sure not to turn away what could potentially be low-hanging or high-hanging fruit. You want to have something for those people, as well. So define your market for your core business, but recognize who your outliers are, and be sure not to turn them away completely. Who knows? Things may shift (as things do in business), and you may end up finding that these are some of your better clients or customers.

Defining your target market can be an arduous process if you aren't completely aware of what you offer. To help you stay focused, create customer personas. This market isn't just filled with fictitious characters on paper—they are real people with real money and real habits. So lay them out. I like to take time to create a customer persona chart so that I can easily refer to it whenever I am creating a campaign, submitting a proposal, pitching services, and performing any other tasks involved in the process. To help you with that, I have included a lovely template for you to use when creating those customer personas. It's very user-friendly and gives you the ability to put a face with a host of characteristics.

Speak to Your Customers; Dialogue with Them

Step 3: Speak to Your Customers; Dialogue with Them

Speaking to your customers is only difficult when you don't know where to find them. Again, this is why Step 1 and Step 2 are so important. Additionally, keep in mind that your target market isn't simply going to wake up in the morning and find you. Make it easy for them to find you, trust you, and understand you by creating multiple search channels. This process, normally known as SEO, can get very complicated, and because of that I have included a list of some quick and easy things you can do to begin this process without having to hire someone to do it immediately.

OK, let's start with my favorite way to communicate with your target market: BLOGGING.

Blogging is an essential way to communicate with the world from your brand's perspective. I get it—who has time to write a blog every week? Well, you do! As a matter of fact, most likely you already have the ideas, the content, and more, but you just haven't take the time to write about it. Oh yeah, and keep in mind that sometimes less is more.

Take some time out and write down some of the things that you have heard recently that relate to what you do. For instance, as a marketing agency, I would write down something like, "I don't know which social media channels to use to promote my business." I have probably said this a million times over to clients, friends, and many others in casual or business conversations but have never taken the time to blog about it. With that, I will take those exact same ideas and opinions that I have bored so many with in conversation and write them down. I will include my opinions in a list of what I think is most efficient, and voila! Just like that, I have a blog.

To keep blogging efficiently, effectively, and consistently, take a few hours a week to do this exact process with about three to four topics. I now have four blog posts a month, and they are already written. Here's the icing on the cake: I can schedule them to post so that I don't have to worry about when they post and take any additional hours out of my day to post them.

Next: social media, social media, social media. (Did I say social media?) Social media is still one of the fastest and most effective ways to communicate with your target market. In this day and age, everyone from your grandmother to your baby sister is on social media for one reason or another. And every day, those individuals are interacting with brands similar to yours.

I am not going to lie to you and say social media is easy to manage. It isn't, and it takes some true work to make it effective and create engagement that will convert to clients.

Here are some steps to help make social media easier to handle.

1. *Research what social media platforms your target market is using*

2. *Create social media channels that are consistent with your brand*
    a. You profile name is important
    b. Your profile picture is even more important
    c. Creating taglines that attract people is crucial

    d. Taking the time to give as much detail in your profile setup is key

OK, now that you have your profiles set up, what are you going to post? Here's where you need to take a second to do some planning and refer back to Step 1 and Step 2. Whom are you trying to reach, what do you want to say, and—most importantly—how will you inspire people to communicate with your brand?

1. *Collect, Create Content*
   a. Set up a standard overlay for pictures, quotes, and other media that will include your brand name, logo, or tagline
   b. Grab your calendar, know what events you are attending, when holidays are, when you are planning to have a sale or special, and don't forget to grab that blog you created.

2. *Create a Social Media Calendar*
   a. Once you have gathered your content (not a one-time process—you will have to do this consistently, because social media is fast-paced, and things change quickly, so make this calendar fluid)
   b. Plan out your posts for each social media channel you intend to use (For example, you will likely post more often to Twitter than Facebook, so you will need to keep track of your content to know what's going where, when, and how often)
   c. The template provided will help you put all of those posts into order by network, create hashtags, and more.

Email Marketing

More than likely, when you started this business you already had a network of friends, business associates, and others who would love to hear about you and your brand. Well, who are you to deny them that opportunity?

Email marketing is a great way to communicate with those potential clients, business associates, and future lovers of you and your brand.

Again, less is more. Don't overwhelm people with emails about your everyday struggles or accomplishments. Keep it short, sweet, and to the point, and use links to allow them to go deeper if they choose.

Send them announcement emails about a new launch and new ways they can reach you (i.e. the social media channels we just launched, the changes to your website, coupons, where they can find your blog—you get the point)

This email is not an attempt to sell them as much as it is to keep them informed. Don't spam them with an email every week (frankly, that's just rude). Ease them in by sending an introductory email introducing your brand, what you stand for, and where they can find you and interact with you, and allow them to opt-in to receive more.

Emails should always be very high level, easy to read, esthetically pleasing, and include a call to action. What do you want them to do after reading this email? Is it buy a product, visit your blog, and take a survey? Whatever it is, ask for it. (A closed mouth doesn't get fed!)

Moving right along…

Make It Easy by Planning

STEP 4: Make It Easy by Planning

All of this can seem so overwhelming at start and can also feel like you just added a zillion things to your already long laundry list of to-dos. Don't let that discourage you—take a deep breath, and do some planning.

Use tools that will keep you efficient and productive. Marketing is not meant to slow down productivity; rather, it is used to create awareness of your brand and be your first line of business development.

With that being said, let's break it down:

1. Use the Brand Audit Template to nail down your target market
2. Use the Customer Persona Template to know your target market
3. Create a blog/editorial calendar for your blog, and schedule your posts through your blog provider
4. Create a social media calendar—the template provided should allow you to drop content in and plan what is going to which network and when

Creating a plan of action will allow you to **Keep Calm and Keep Marketing** (You see what I did there? LOL). The last thing anyone wants is to be overwhelmed by one more thing, and the reality is that you probably opened this business to give you more freedom eventually. Don't buy another job. Planning will allow you to have the ability to walk away and move to something else without worry that things will fail.

Put things on Auto-Pilot

Step 5: Put Things on Auto-Pilot (Know your destination, and get there without having to have your hand on the wheel at all times)

In short, automate your marketing efforts! Marketing automation provides you with the tools necessary to reach, engage, and respond to your customers/clients in a timely, well-planned, and strategically arranged manner.

Or, if all of this is still too much, you could always hire a marketer (*hint, hint*).

But, in all seriousness, take the time to automate so that you can focus your energies now on converting those leads, producing more wonderful products, or enjoying a little moment of free time.

1. Get publishing software for social media—take a look at the list provided, and choose which one works best for you
2. Schedule your emails in advance through email marketing software
3. Schedule you blog posts to go out every week at the same time

Use the tools provided in this book, or create your own—it's completely up to you. But if you do not automate, you will become overwhelmed. Marketing is not a one-time deal. It's ongoing and ever-changing. Automation is also not meant to set and forget; you will need to assess what's working and what's not working, which brings me to the next step.

It's Necessary to Analyze, Take Notes, and Refocus

Step 6: It's Necessary to Analyze, Take Notes, and Refocus

I am not writing this book to provide you with a means to set up your marketing and leave it to do the work. I simply want to provide you with a few tools that will help get you started and keep you focused. But, as always, we must be introspective in life and in business. Everything isn't going to go as planned, and marketing isn't magic. It is a process of always gaining a clearer understanding of the needs and wants of your clients/customers. It's much like an *Eat, Pray, Love* journey. (OK, maybe not that dramatic, but you get the point.)

In this step, it's time do some real work. Oh, you didn't think everything could be so simple, did you? Marketing efforts have to be analyzed and reworked at times. The most important thing you can do for your business is take time to look at the analytics. Find out what's working and what's not. So often I talk to business owners, and they are overwhelmed because they have implemented all of the steps, and yet nothing is working. Well, when I told you that Step 1 and Step 2 were going to be the most crucial in all of this, I meant it.

When you look at your efforts, the content created, the posts made, and the emails sent, I want you to look at the analytics. How many people opened your email? Did they click on the links? How long were they on your blog? How long did they read your email?

All of these things matter.

Don't get mad at the numbers—not all numbers are going to be through the roof. In the beginning, we are looking for consistent small growth.

So let me break it down. When it comes to email marketing, the average open rates (according to industries) are as follows:

Industry	Open Rate	Click Rate	Soft Bounce Rate
Beauty & Personal Care	20.72%	2.82%	0.82%
Retail	23.16%	3.26%	0.66%
Consulting	18.78%	2.57%	1.76%
Arts/Artists	27.97%	3.28%	1.17%

Statistics credit: Mail Chimp (http://mailchimp.com/resources/research/email-marketing-benchmarks/)

Don't get upset if you see similar numbers, because that's actually a good thing. This means your email is working.

Social media analytics all have very different meanings according to the channel you are using.

Here are a few things you want to take a look at on social media.

1. Conversion Rate: The conversion rate is the percentage of visitors who take desired actions on a website—how many visitors took the time to take action by clicking on your blog link, website link, etc.

2. Engagement Rate: the engagement rate is a metric that allows you to benchmark content performance based on audience interaction. Likes, shares, and follows are key performance indicators here. (This number is a consistent calculation but can vary often, so be sure to measure its growth and consistency over time, as it is not a sum total of what's happening). Last, but certainly not least, we need to find some benchmarks. A simple formula to use to find benchmarks in social media is the following: **(Total engagements [comments, likes, and shares]/total fans) x 100 = avg. page engagement rate**

3. Reach: You need to know how many people you are reaching to understand your true imprint, but take it a step further, and drill in on who these people are. Measure that up against who is engaging with you to see if the people you are reaching are actually a part of your target market. Make some notes about what's happening over time so that you can make informed decisions when making changes to things.

OK, OK, I know that was a lot. Well rest easy, because most of the social media platforms have these analytics built in, and when you are using the social media publishing tools, make sure to choose one with these monitoring features. This will make life a lot easier for you.

Before we say "goodbye," there is one last step.

Always Be Closing (Analyze, Pitch, Close)

Step 7: Always Be Closing (Analyze, Pitch, Close)

I don't care what business you are in—you have to talk to people. Social media, digital strategies, and many other assets will continue to assist in the growth of your business, but that will only bring people to the table. It is your job to feed them.

So here's my last word: If you are looking for ways to grow your business, you must be strategic. After all, now you know exactly what you do and whom you want to work with based on the work we did upfront. So, here is what I want you to do. Create a Top 10 List. This list consists of the top 10 clients or customers you want. Analyze that customer/client, find the pain in his or her current state, and exploit it. (But make sure you do this in a cordial way. Don't run around calling people's babies ugly—I am not responsible for you getting slapped!)

But, seriously, you know your product or service fills a gap for them. Write down a high-level explanation of why your product or service belongs with them. Here's the start of your pitch. Be gracious in your pitch—again, you want to congratulate them on the success thus far and let them know you are truly a fan. Then explain to them in a normal way (not a hard sales-y way) why you think your product or service will be perfect for them. Don't forget that pain. Remember I said exploit it. Here's your chance let them know you have done your research and see a fit. Give them the quick and dirty "I noticed you don't have XYZ, and I know my company loves to help in this area." Reel them in with kindness and fact. Now that you have their attention, ask them for more time.

Lastly, it's time to close. Ask for the business, partnership, and placement in stores and wherever else you desire. Don't be afraid of "NO." It usually means "not right now" in most cases, and it gives you the opportunity to follow up at a later date.

Continue to go after opportunities, and let all of the work you have done in marketing your business support those efforts. In some cases, those efforts might also not even be needed, because clients and customers may approach, ready and willing.

FINALLY, REPEAT!

That's it—repeat these steps for any new products and services. I pray this was helpful to you. Please feel free to use all of the templates, provided lists, and any other resources useful to you. If you are going through the process and questions arrive, please email me at jamila.guyton@prosyncconsulting.com, and I will be glad to coach you through any one of the steps. Visit www.prosyncconsulting.com for more great tips, and stay tuned for our next book: *Create a Revenue Funnel*. Never have just one stream of income or one level of products and services.

Appendix A: Brand Audit Template

BRAND AUDIT TEMPLATE				
ProSync Consulting				
COMPANY VIEW				
HIGH LEVEL STRATEGIC ALIGNMENT				
Component	Description	Question Answered	Factors	Implications
Strategic Alignment	Describes where the firm is going, how it will get there, and who the firm is.	Are we aligned in terms of resources and direction with the overall corporate direction?	◆ Vision ◆ Mission ◆ Business Sustainability ◆ Brand Strategy ◆ Marketing Objectives	◆ Brand alignment assures that the brand is supportive of the overall direction of the firm ◆ Brand misalignment is an indication that the brand is working at cross purposes to the direction of the firm
COMPETITION				
Component	Description	Question Answered	Factors	Implications
Competition	Identifies those firms which offer brands similar to ours in the eyes of the customer.	How do our brands compare to our competitors? What is the potential for competitive differentiation?	◆ Brand Architecture ◆ Brands ◆ Differentiation ◆ Market ◆ Personality ◆ Positioning ◆ Segments	◆ Understanding how the brand compares to the competition is important as it provides guidance for our brand strategy in terms of the directions to take.
BRAND				
Component	Description	Question Answered	Factors	Implications
Brand Architecture	Describes the nature of the relationship between different brands.	Is the emphasis on the individual brand(s) or a master brand?	◆ Brand House ◆ House of Brands	◆ Uncoordinated architecture is an indication that some of the brands may not be properly supported
Brand Strategy	Defines the purpose of the brand in the eyes of the company.	Where does the brand fit into the overall marketing strategy?	◆ Cash Cow ◆ Corporate ◆ Distinguisher ◆ Fighter ◆ Flagship ◆ Strategic	◆ A poor brand strategy fails to properly support branding and marketing investments ◆ Poor branding strategy fails to signal the view of the brand by the firm
Brand Role	Describes the function of the brand with respect to other brands.	What role does the brand play?	◆ Co-Driver ◆ Driver ◆ Endorser ◆ Extension ◆ Ingredient ◆ Sub Brand	◆ Definition of the role of the brand serves to indicate its relative contribution to equity and assists in allocating resources and naming. ◆ A poorly defined role is indicative of a poor overall brand strategy
Touch Points	Are the points at which the customer comes into contact with the brand?	Where does the customer come into contact with the brand?	◆ Channel ◆ Communications ◆ Customer Service ◆ Logo	◆ Understanding the touch points of the brand for the customer is essential to understanding the customer's view of the brand.

				◆ Packaging	
				◆ Price	
				◆ Product	
				◆ Website	

MARKET

Component	Description	Question Answered	Factors	Implications
Customer	Defines the customer profile.	Who is the customer?		◆ The better the definition of the customer the more precise the marketing efforts to support the brand
Market	Defines the total group of potential customers for the brand.	What is the potential for the brand?	◆ Accessible ◆ Buying Practices ◆ Identified ◆ Maturity Level ◆ Profiled ◆ Sufficient ◆ Trends	◆ Effective market definition serves to indicate the potential for the brand and supports marketing investment decisions ◆ Poor market definition fails to identify the brands potential and leads to potential misallocation of marketing resources
Segmentation	What market segments have been identified for the brand?	What are the characteristics of the different customers for the brand?	◆ Behavioral ◆ Demographic ◆ Geographic ◆ Interest based ◆ Psychographic	◆ Strong segmentation assists in the development of the marketing communications and marketing investment allocations for the brand
Target	Identifies which customers to focus on within the market segments.	What customers represent the most value for the brand?	◆ Concentrated ◆ Differentiated ◆ Undifferentiated	◆ Strong targeting assists in the development of the marketing communications and marketing investment

BRAND SUPPORT STRATEGY

Creative Strategy	Describes the overall approach	What are the key points to promote with respect to the brand?	◆ Linked to positioning statement	◆ Misalignment of the creative strategy with the brand strategy results in ineffective marketing communications
Content Strategy	Identifies the subject matter and tools for use in content development related to the brand.	What are we going to say and where are we going to say it?	◆ Creation ◆ Governance ◆ Publication	◆ Lack of proper content management can lead to dissolution of the brand message

MEASURMENT

Component	Description	Question Answered	Factors	Implications
Metrics	Measures used to evaluate the effectiveness of current brand strategy.	How are we doing with regard to managing the brand?	◆ Image ◆ Impact ◆ Market Share ◆ Profitability ◆ Revenue	◆ Measuring brand parameters provides an indication as to the success of the brand management efforts

CUSTOMER VIEW

Component	Description	Question Answered	Factors	Implications

Personality	Identifies the characteristics associated with the brand.	How does the customer view the brand?	♦ Competence ♦ Excitement ♦ Ruggedness ♦ Sincerity ♦ Sophistication (Based Aaker Model)	♦ Alignment of the firms view of the brand personality with that of the customers is one indication of effective brand management ♦ Misalignment conversely indicates a disconnect between the firms brand management and the customer
Decision Criteria	On what basis will purchasers of the brand make their decisions?	How do customers decide to buy our brand?	♦ Convenience ♦ Emotional ♦ Functional ♦ Price	♦ Understanding as to the decision criteria allows for the marketing efforts to be aligned with the decision criteria and support the brand
Competitive Differentiation	Describes how we are different from the competition.	What makes the brand unique?	♦ Valuable ♦ Rare ♦ Imitatible ♦ Organized (VRIO Model)	♦ The more differentiated the brand is from the competition the stronger its' positioning in the eyes of the customer ♦ Poor differentiation means that customers fail to see the value in our brand positioning potentially leading to commodity status
Positioning	Describes where we want the brand to be in the minds of the customer.	How do we want the market to perceive the brand?	♦ Brand Fit ♦ Credibility ♦ Customer Relevance ♦ Sustainability ♦ Uniqueness	♦ Strong positioning serves to help differentiate the brand in the mind of the customer ♦ Weak positioning leads to commoditization
Influencers	Identifies who are the outside individuals or groups that have power with respect to the brand?	Who else is defining the brand?	♦ Brand links shared ♦ Content preferred	♦ Recognizing that control of the brand rests largely with the customer understanding who influences the customer, and in what manner, assures that the firms marketing efforts are not counter to those of the customer
Communities	Defines the profile for the groups associated with the brand.	What communities are associated with the brand?	♦ Content preferred	♦ Communities tied to brands have a powerful voice in determining what the brand stands for making it imperative to understand their view of the brand and align with it.
Equity	Identifies the perceived value of the brand.	What is the brand worth?	♦ Brand Imagery ♦ Brand Performance ♦ Customer Feelings ♦ Customer Judgment ♦ Prominence ♦ Resonance	♦ Measuring brand equity provides a high level valuation of the marketing efforts to support the brand

Persona Name

BACKGROUND:
- Basic details about persona's role
- Key information about the persona's company
- Relevant background info, like education or hobbies

DEMOGRAPHICS:
- Gender
- Age Range
- HH Income (Consider a spouse's income, if relevant)
- Urbanicity (Is your persona urban, suburban, or rural?)

IDENTIFIERS:
- Buzz words
- Mannerisms

You can find this information by administering online surveys of your target audience.

Appendix C: Social Media Publishing Template * create a tab like this for each Social Network*

DAY	DATE	TIME	DATE & TIME	UPDATE COPY	LINK	TRACKING TOKEN
MONDAY						
	1/5/2015	9:00:00	05/01/2015 09:00			
	1/5/2015	12:00:00	05/01/2015 12:00			
	1/5/2015	15:00:00	05/01/2015 15:00			
	1/5/2015	17:00:00	05/01/2015 17:00			
TUESDAY						
	1/6/2015	9:00:00	06/01/2015 09:00	Inspiration		
	1/6/2015	12:00:00	06/01/2015 12:00			
	1/6/2015	15:00:00	06/01/2015 15:00			
	1/6/2015	17:00:00	06/01/2015 17:00			
WEDNESDAY						
	1/7/2015	9:00:00	07/01/2015 09:00			
	1/7/2015	12:00:00	07/01/2015 12:00			
	1/7/2015	15:00:00	07/01/2015 15:00			
	1/7/2015	17:00:00	07/01/2015 17:00			
THURSDAY						
	1/8/2015	9:00:00	08/01/2015 09:00			
	1/8/2015	12:00:00	08/01/2015 12:00			
	1/8/2015	15:00:00	08/01/2015 15:00			
	1/8/2015	17:00:00	08/01/2015 17:00			
FRIDAY						
	1/9/2015	9:00:00	09/01/2015 09:00			
	1/9/2015	12:00:00	09/01/2015 12:00			
	1/9/2015	15:00:00	09/01/2015 15:00			
	1/9/2015	17:00:00	09/01/2015 17:00			
SATURDAY						
	1/10/2015	9:00:00	10/01/2015 09:00			
	1/10/2015	12:00:00	10/01/2015 12:00			
	1/10/2015	15:00:00	10/01/2015 15:00			
	1/10/2015	17:00:00	10/01/2015 17:00			
SUNDAY						
	1/11/2015	9:00:00	11/01/2015 09:00			
	1/11/2015	12:00:00	11/01/2015 12:00			
	1/11/2015	15:00:00	11/01/2015 15:00			
	1/11/2015	17:00:00	11/01/2015 17:00			

Appendix D: Blog Editorial Calendar

ProSync CONSULTING		TOPIC/TITLE	CONTENT/DETAILS	KEYWORD(S)	TARGET PERSONA(S)	OFFER/CTA
MONDAY						
Author:						
Due Date:	10/20/2015					
Publish Date:	10/23/2015					
TUESDAY						
Author:						
Due Date:	10/20/2015					
Publish Date:	10/23/2015					
WEDNESDAY						
Author:						
Due Date:	10/20/2015					
Publish Date:	10/23/2015					
THURSDAY						
Author:						
Due Date:						
Publish Date:						
FRIDAY						
Author:						
Due Date:						
Publish Date:						
SATURDAY						
Author:						
Due Date:						
Publish Date:						
SUNDAY						
Author:						
Due Date:						
Publish Date:						

www.ingramcontent.com/pod-product-compliance
Lightning Source LLC
Chambersburg PA
CBHW041616180526
45159CB00002BC/887